PENGUIN BOOKS

NERVOUS SYSTEMS

WILLIAM STOBB lives in La Crosse, Wisconsin, where he is professor of English at Viterbo University. He was the winner of the Nevada Arts Council Poetry Fellowship for 2000, and his poems have appeared in *American Poetry Review*, *Denver Quarterly*, and *Colorado Review*. His reviews and commentary appear regularly on miPOradio.

THE NATIONAL POETRY SERIES

The National Poetry Series was established in 1978 to ensure the publication of five poetry books annually through participating publishers. Publication is funded by the Lannan Foundation: Stephen Graham; Joyce & Seward Johnson Foundation; Glenn Schaeffer; Juliet Lea Hillman Simonds Foundation; Tiny Tiger Foundation; and Charles B. Wright III. This project also is supported in part by an award from the National Endowment for the Arts, which believes that a great nation deserves great art.

2006 COMPETITION WINNERS

Laynie Browne of Oakland, California, *The Scented Fox*
Chosen by Alice Notley, to be published by Wave Books

Noah Eli Gordon of Denver, Colorado, *Novel Pictorial Noise*
Chosen by John Ashbery, to be published by HarperCollins

Laurie Clements Lambeth of Houston, Texas, *Veil and Burn*
Chosen by Maxine Kumin, to be published by University of
    Illinois Press

Martha Ronk of Los Angeles, California, *Vertigo*
Chosen by C. D. Wright, to be published by Coffee House Press

William Stobb of La Crosse, Wisconsin, *Nervous Systems*
Chosen by August Kleinzahler, to be published by Penguin Books

NERVOUS SYSTEMS

WILLIAM STOBB

PENGUIN BOOKS

PENGUIN BOOKS

Published by the Penguin Group

Penguin Group (USA) Inc., 375 Hudson Street, New York, New York 10014, U.S.A.

Penguin Group (Canada), 90 Eglinton Avenue East, Suite 700, Toronto, Ontario, Canada
M4P 2Y3 (a division of Pearson Penguin Canada Inc.)

Penguin Books Ltd, 80 Strand, London WC2R 0RL, England

Penguin Ireland, 25 St Stephen's Green, Dublin 2, Ireland (a division of Penguin Books Ltd)

Penguin Group (Australia), 250 Camberwell Road, Camberwell, Victoria 3124, Australia
(a division of Pearson Australia Group Pty Ltd)

Penguin Books India Pvt Ltd, 11 Community Centre, Panchsheel Park,
New Delhi – 110 017, India

Penguin Group (NZ), 67 Apollo Drive, Rosedale, North Shore 0745, Auckland, New Zealand
(a division of Pearson New Zealand Ltd.)

Penguin Books (South Africa) (Pty) Ltd, 24 Sturdee Avenue, Rosebank, Johannesburg 2196,
South Africa

Penguin Books Ltd, Registered Offices:
80 Strand, London WC2R 0RL, England

First published in Penguin Books 2007

1 3 5 7 9 10 8 6 4 2

Page iv constitutes an extension of this copyright page.

LIBRARY OF CONGRESS CATALOGING IN PUBLICATION DATA
Stobb, William.
Nervous systems / William Stobb.
p. cm.—(National poetry series)
ISBN 978-0-14-311199-3
I. Title.
PS3619.T625N47 2007
811'.6—dc22 2006052798

Printed in the United States of America
Set in Granjon
Designed by Ginger Legato

Thanks to friends, some who have helped me with these poems
and some who have just helped me: Doran Wright, Nick
Plunkey, Marc Lundeen, Deborah Bernhardt, David Krump,
Kelly Sexton, Andy Moore, Anna Krause, Penny Libel,
and Mitch Reynolds.

Thanks to my mentors and teachers, Brenda Hillman, Donald
Revell, Claudia Keelan, and Jay Meek.

Special thanks to all my family, but especially to Claire and
Carter, who inspire me every day.

This book is dedicated to Kari Houser.

ACKNOWLEDGMENTS

Thanks to the following periodicals, for printing poems from this collection, and for permission to reprint those poems:

American Literary Review: "At the Afterlife Hotel"
Babylon Burning: 9/11 five years on: "A History of Interruption"
Catalyst: "Poem with Hard Thinking" and "In a Corner"
Colorado Review: "Tower with Beach or Basin," "Poem in the Food Chain," "Inside +/− Outside," and "The Subway Portraits"
Denver Quarterly: "*Rhenish*" and "Time Is Going Down in Me"
donga: "Poem with Too Many Worlds" and "Sin Ten Million"
Interim: "Other Exposure" and "I Put Up a Trellis"
Kiosk: "The Cellist"
Midwest Poetry Review: "Failed Survey" (as "Midland Survey")
MiPOesias: "Poem for Detroit," "Crow," "Manifest," and "Poem after People Die"
Neon: "Pose"
North Dakota Quarterly: "Five Years after Watching the Perseids with a Friend"
Revista Atenea: "Nervous Systems" and "Other Greens. Reductions."
Southwestern American Literature: "An Absurd Film"
Three Candles: "Circa Oh Two," "For Real June," and "October with Zoloft Trial Packet"
Touchstone: "Fugue" and "'We Could Live Here'"
Wisconsin Academy Review: "For Hearing and Not Hearing"
"Five Years after Watching the Perseids with a Friend" appears as a broadside printed by Carol J. Waldren, commissioned by the Black Rock Press Broadside Competition.
Some of these poems appear in the limited-edition chapbook *For Better Night Vision* (Black Rock Press, 2000).
"The New Development" was awarded the Thomas McGrath Prize by the Academy of American Poets.
This project has been funded, in part, by a grant from the Nevada Arts Council, a state agency, and the National Endowment for the Arts, a federal agency.

CONTENTS

BLANK SYSTEM

NERVOUS SYSTEMS

A scorpion pins and then injects
a moth with fluorescent venom.
A man in a lab coat explains: impulses
accelerate for one mad second
before total paralysis—
"What we would call death."

Another tech massages a monkey frog
with an electrode. On its bright
green skin appears a creamy venom
that slows AIDS in serum.
The scientist strokes the frog absentmindedly.
He says it enjoys the process.

I remember the view from Mt. Rose peak—
the alpine lake and north-south range.
Nevada to the east in yellow and brown waves.
I sensed charged filaments in my eyes.
Streams could almost be seen
as strands of wire entering me.

Here's a patterned view of river valley weather:
twenty-nine smokestacks twirl a sky necklace
in flow over flow. Out of Calgary
a cool trough spins the chain along the Great Lakes.
A spiral line eyes the Atlantic.
This hour: a new foot of snow for New York.

+ / −

I'd been reading about the homunculus—
the little man inside translating the body
into the world—when I noticed light taps
on the loose panes of this screened patio.

I'd been preoccupied with the friend
not wanting to get married but getting
married in a month, in Maine.
My eyes came up from the page.

The azalea's budding. It's May.
And then the light taps of rain.
I heard and smelled and saw and stood

and left that other worry
to enter weather's worry.
It felt so good outside.

WING SYSTEM

How soon unaccountable I became

Walt Whitman

POEM IN THE FOOD CHAIN

Happens I get a mile down
some single track and worry:
no one knows I'm hiking.
Trail skirts constant blind rustling in
knee-high thistle.
Flies slap my head then circle.
Seven bears per mile square: who
said that? Brother? Store clerk?
Hold still
one minute.
Breathe.
Sunlight in a clearing thirty yards left—
I'm certain it's the river.
Up from the ground a slim bark chip flutters
under my chin.
I flinch.
Its wings open blue.

OCTOBER WITH ZOLOFT TRIAL PACKET

It got surprisingly hot for one hour

Bees resumed streaking like flaring
Points and grass became

Intensely bright
Easy thinking this bright

Wild neighborhood air
Its own galaxy in the galaxy

So sunny I sneezed repeatedly

When seasonal patterns regained control

One wasp between pane and screen
Never moved while I

Read that poem again about
Wasting summer life in

A hammock
Is it ungrateful

Season wanting to die

Wasp never moves
While stanzas go down

A cold front crosses the bluff

Now grim outside I
Hereby predict sleet

All the bees unwound October
And decelerated I guess

They're finished

Then the rear left the longest of six

Legs detached from the
Screen swung

Out the thorax trailing slow
Rotated and the front

Right leg ticked one screen-
Square to straighten the

Bee

MANIFEST

Twelve thousand versions of twelve dozen ivy blossoms
in the compound eye
                of a dragonfly

          Shoulder-wide
crevice opens above a gravel run
                     bottles
      and a condom we decided
not to touch
part of the preserve

                Grove of future dirt
surrounds a cluster of brightly
clothed children   One
             as they say
         is mine

Near the scout shelter along the tracks
a woodpecker harvested termites
from the decaying limb of an ash
                  Sawdust
              sprinkled over
          the sumac's beseeching leaves
Idea's that
we're getting what birds are just doing?
        Who drew that
  white line

             on the sky?
      Mine's spied
the day's first vapor trail—
passenger plane on the hop to Chicago

                              By nine
                          it's diffused
               combined with others of its kind
   and high cirrus
                        One white charge
   snaps through made weather

                         Twelve thousand versions
                      of twelve dozen blossoms
   in the compound eye

POEM WITH HARD THINKING

Maybe birds are complaining
in the junk elm along the trestle.
Singing is just an idea.

It's not sick to think this way. Relax.
In art class I used pudding
to paint mountains. In Phys. Ed.
I showered in my clothes.

Now I'm inventing bird therapy
where trains pass—they're so fast because
the world swelled and everything's farther.

A fast train can only end the fizzle
sizzle inside a bad birdie.
The little bird body goes on
pinned to the outbound express.

CROW

for Kevin Marzahl

Ride bike fast and slow   like even
people on the paved trail
by the tracks and in neighborhoods   like odd
                  half-glimpsed
houses and curb-shaped stripes of yellow
                 ball flies up
      above the tree these children play
ball at the very edge of traffic
having no safe concept   casual
             neighborhood

crimes slide past
even the president bet
the have-not kind
in casual households
make out like a crow   finds a bat sleeping
        under a buckled shingle
      he rips away
four rapid beak attacks
change one bat from old to new
dark   halfway to Stoddard
on the highway trail
too toothy smiles on the fronts of
too fast Broncos   ride fast   flat-out dive
down the switchyard access road
north past the trailer park   saving my life
circle stop one minute   friend told me
at the outskirt fountain   crank pedals
then on along this rim   go crow

"WE COULD LIVE HERE"

for Kari Houser

1.

Age four and her backseat
ideas seem very real: a nine-hour drive
to the grandparents' lake
she makes a new incarnation out the window.

We drive north into late pine light.
A minivan easily climbs a moraine.
On the shoulders crows preside
over any number of corpses per mile.

She sits too low for body count.
Her landscape's innocent
canopy and distance.
Behind the wheel
I tick, worry, scan ditches
for any glimmer.

2.

After morning fishing, we make the Red Carpet—
one of a dozen northern resorts
where men in fishnet hats drink coffee 'til noon then Miller.

Laid off from industrial welding
the owner's daughter's trying
to tend bar and also install a new water pump
in the broken-down Ford out front.

She hustles back and forth, greasy
towel in hand. She takes a minute
and tells us about the local who
followed a Karner blue
into trees behind his cabin.
Three days later found the county road.
Three months later sees blue flutter.

That night we mistake an island fire for a lake accident.
Thinking someone there will know the details
we call the Red Carpet and the sheriff's at the bar.
Kari describes the flame, maybe
eight miles out: it dims

then explodes again like a new fuel line's been ignited.
Sheriff knows nada. Turns out
it's a brush fire in the Northwest Angle
burns all the next day
and we slept imagining bodies in the water.

3.

Walking the beach on the day we're leaving
daughter picks up a water-worn bottle shard.
Water's full of glass. Ha.

I want her to know it's touched by mystery
fragile, formerly
dangerous, risen transformed.
But I suspect it's another collectible.

We scramble across a deadfall
she finds the bleached-clean skull
of a good-sized pike. *Can I keep these bones?*
I say she can keep the bottle.

Driving home I watch her sleep
in the rearview—her eyes work through
another world of items for saving.

POEM AFTER PEOPLE DIE

Squinting up in the dim last of it
I think I recognize the makings
of the new nest in the lilac

Clothing torn off an old mannequin
(not a mannequin but I can't say the body's name)
shredded by starlings   starlings
beyond a wire fence   know a figure
gone cold   starlings know dead
          and fake

I recognize this feeling: indignant
When did these rights concepts open in me?
Got to feeling like something   someone   just because
I like it doesn't
mean it's supposed to keep existing

One hard fall winter spring
everyone's someone dies and everyone
smiles through but it's crazy smiling

Gets dark   birds stop   every single night
I read letters in the orange recliner   (letters can
The boy comes down   spell knot in
out of sleep   a way that means no
making lovely sounds   tangled and bound)
like *swim swim* and smiling in
two worlds

I'll try to sleep   try to remember new summer
at the public pool   everyone's new standing
at the edge the water really   is blue and you
really can go   down in the cold and open
                                see

EXPOSED SYSTEM

What a million filaments

Sylvia Plath

TOWER WITH BEACH OR BASIN

The dune in the photo is almost the dune
in the east window
where any scape inspires fearful dreams—a range,

a ruin, a trembling sleep.

Tenant threatens to reveal
building's old pipes; super pretends to hammer them,
smoking drugs, collecting on drugs.

With the rains, the odor

of resin settles from the desert air. With the heat
people break free of the time line—
a bipolar super stifling all resident claims.

If it were mysterious

the ocean would never arrive here, or
have arrived.
The tower in the photo would simply be a new tower, the dune

the same but older

no longer inching forth, just hung there by a stilled wind.
Sense the image in perpetuity
and contact defers, what with the memory of every

scent and texture, every delirium

associated in the new language of desire with sand.

The sea marks the playa with an *X*.

The super burns the photo. Pipes rattle through

the long night while new systems advance.

POSE

J. propped photos in the full fruit basket.
N. hosted guests in the next room. Next
N. tried looking like a man not diminished.
J. crossed Evans, jacket slung, vodka dangling.

Spontaneity—I've since heard it defined as a present
moment suspending actions across space

like photos of beautiful things
they did to each other in the moments when they cared.
She left them slightly overexposed
among the limes, so his best friends could see

all he's got, stilled and glaring, while he
stood shaking, hosting a party at his own epicenter.

Blink—she's out the door not exactly gone just gone
elsewhere with her large desires.
The evidence—her brash presence
in the stills, pressed up against everything, snarling

into his red eyes. Sitting on the counter
in the wake of it

he said he made lemon dessert the first time
she stayed over. He learned they were fragile
and explosive, each a striking
match at the point of flare / snap.

It's like a pose, I began, meaning to say *possession*
but feeling the *e* vaporize as S. began handling

the pears, swinging her hips. L. slid up behind her
and they teased everything out. After all
festivities will resume, though doors in the house
open and close, signs flash, like the Don't

Walk sign on Evans where many cars pass
but only one honks

at the sexy pedestrian slugging vodka in the crosswalk.

Shutter open and not Vegas exploding
in last light of dusk.

Shutter open and not sky elapsing.
Not flowers
bursting open with the over-
the-top sexual beauty
of their elapsing.

Shutter open on range.
The Pollock action stain
of time (red) on tectonics.

In the Valley of Fire
dead afternoon
one I know was lost.

He set the shutter open on himself and stared.
When voices shouted
he was saved

nothing ever closed.
A tall young man with work and lovers
living near the seam
where desert opened from sea, living up
against clear bright.

AN ABSURD FILM

Black Rock Desert
(for Francis Fritz)

        The way we continually miss each other
it's as if long segments had been cut. *I looked*
at the stars last night my character pronounces
and I don't know where we are. A long pause ensues.
I think of a chemistry lab—electrons arranged
like planets in an unfamiliar system.
                           Remember the
party? you respond. *The woman with no headdress?*
I want that party. It's not a different story. It's denial.
I touch your robe in a gesture of consolation. We speculate
about rescue
                walking hopeless miles of windblown playa.
In my life, the plant on my kitchen table
reminded me spilling from its pot of someone's
hair I never dared touch and the curve
in the neck of a brass swan holding a candle
made me in love.
               You dream of rain
shoot awake sensing a mouth on your stomach
unable to stop yourself.
                  Is it you? Me?
I turn in circles. The same dry land
the same mountains we imagined were stern faces.
The same the same the same.

X

Fire. Last light
carving shards of black on the valley floor.
No longer filming, we remember not to limp
not to pretend we're surprised by the motion of the air
and a sense of slipping we invented as a metaphor.
Pampered, futuristic humans
survivors of a crash
                              barefoot on a desert playa.
Playa. Playa. One never tires of saying it I've found.
Even in the future we spoke of it dramatically.
This playa is cursed this playa
is long and barren and wide and this playa
is where we will die.
                    I put it on my tongue
playing my role, imagining lovers and survival.

X

                    Weeks after dying of thirst as planned
I stood in the darkened hallway of a turn-of-the-century
administrative building and spoke the word firmly
listened to my many voices.
                    A friend heard me
came from her room and touched my arm. For a moment
her footsteps were audible and I could smell the desert.
For a moment light graced
                    the cinder block walls.

Once when I had been young so long ago my parents
had taken me to the edge of a body
of stagnant water with lights and faces in it
telling me of a people whose children
                              were drowned
to prevent a great storm. We danced. I was immersed.
Speaking of this and tired from a day of walking
I would gaze across the playa and simply stop
lie down and exchange stories with that new wind.

Mark Rothko gives his copy of *The Trial*
to a girl he wants to sleep with.
She must be overcast and threatening.
In any case threatening. In any case it works.

To commemorate what passes between them
he paints outdoor figures
gazing at the sea.

The subway scenes make more sense to me.
Nervous glances between passengers
premonition of something sharp flashing out
and in fact he uses a knife to make the people thin.

In full exposure, I can't believe the figures.
The sea's like a cartoon—
ha ha time, ha ha vanishing point.

"For a while I was with a really numb one.
In a drive-through, he tore up a card
he'd carried for a decade and said that was it:
no more caring about that or any other attachments even
to me. No more harmless elevation
of small things like weather or a nice flower
to the status of material. Nothing
would from then on concern him.
Then we took our tacos and he politely
asked the attendant to dispose of the many pieces of his card.
I liked the way he did that."

"In the new empty world
my daydreaming became excessive.
I often pictured bodies with many
engines like cartoon cyclones in the torso.
I heard about killings on the news
and imagined these tight spirals
twisting down, dividing, streaking away.
It's a feeble kind of grasping and I'm ashamed.
I remember the card was a regular business card
yellowed and thinning with some printing.
What it said was 'totally irrelevant.' I guess
I admired him. He seemed
so definite compared to almost everyone."

POEM WITH TOO MANY WORLDS

after Henry Darger

K. complains: everyone now
wears khakis with a solid color T-shirt.
It's his way of denouncing the era
which is nothing for him—he mostly occupies
an enormous inner world of objects broken
down to parts. No surprise
he whips me at pool, which is where we are now:
playing pool all Friday afternoon
at Ray's Bar and Grill. In the past
I worked for Ray, selling tables, cues, and supplies
out of a west side warehouse. Once
he sent me upstairs to pull a catalog from his desk drawer.
When I opened it I saw his billy club
which maybe he wanted me to see.
That didn't stop me from ripping him off, though, occasionally,
and, bold or stupid, ogling his trophy wife, Rebecca.
See, Ray is larger than his bar and grill,
greater than his warehouse, archetypal
in his no-fucking-around-ness and the thuggish
criminal air he exudes. I found his billy club and still
imagined Rebecca in terms of possible copy room affairs—
attractive, friendly, she knew her slates and cushions—
combination school-teacher-slash-Reno-mafia-wife.
It worked in some way on me.
A couple years after I quit, they found
an inoperable tumor and she died within the month.
Now K. denounces the era
while systematically dismantling me in nine ball.
He recedes to the arcade, where *The Vivian Girls*—
the new game of paramilitary Orphan Annies
battling cosmic forces of evil—

draws out the broad array
of his analytical skill and dexterity.
I can't tell you how strange it is
this weekday, three beers down to classic rock
over sizzling fryers, teenagers on vacation
breaking racks, talking smack.
Objects in motion scatter and bank,
an index of all the theories and what a sense
you get, watching a really good player
that an even stroke and clean strike
can keep it entirely under control. In the arcade
K. dominates with full presence. Little girls
like scouts or candy stripers shovel
hot coals down the gullets of pedophiles.
They devise an aircraft from pill bottles
scavenged from dumpsters and fly up
to battle Darger in the clouds.
He's given them penises and they want to understand.
He's afraid and lashes out.
If the girls can help him sleep the game ends
and the player is immortalized in Darger's dream sequence:
the darling survivors dash across a meadow
singing their true names into the distance.
If K. gets that far, I'll be very drunk,
waiting for Ray to come in because
bold or stupid, I need to talk to him.
These disturbing games are his—
these innocent players and attractive frames: even flowers
on the Game Over screen. Rebecca,
I meant no disrespect. Ray,
if it'll make you feel better
you can go get your club now.

High Plains car chase game
                              Race to connect
with isolated storms running the horizon
                        Drive state
highways county roads
any old dirt track to get your   self right
                              in weather
Once I hit washboard at seventy
my Olds leapt
from one gravel edge to the other
                              The steep margin
had a kind of gravity and I understood
I would be found after some time
                              One artist
cast every part of a wrecked American
sedan   reassembled it without the death
            One less
rollover-in-rain-then-bleed-out-humming-the-Supremes
-death   (or one
              more not-that)
                              This blond
Montana kid I knew played trumpet
with the Temptations in Bozeman
                        past their prime
they stepped off the tour bus
in red velvet suits & did groove
                        See how wherever
                              else it goes
                        out and out
it reaches Detroit
                  To fall
through automotion into new music

                                        Air's made
for Motown   Air gets everything down
                                to its pump   broken
                          valve   pooling fluids
                        eventually
              first hard drops
smack the smoking
chassis   Or
                   If
it never does rain maybe a bird   what the
wind sounds like blown over cooling
                                  The point of chasing
storms is to meet before being
unmade   one weather one car
                      one body
                        me as in meteorology
                    If you ever play and win
get out of the car
let the cold rain hammer you some

OTHER GREENS. REDUCTIONS.

"The bulk of distances, the mounds of home."
LYN HEJINIAN, "THE GREEN"

Starting when I am young, concern for the family yard
in summer: thinning, burning
out to its reedy margin. Concern against yellow
breeds these disjointed . . . what. What?
Every morning it's there, the yard, for tending
and inside, at arm's length
a sense that someone's in the garage
drinking coffee, dissatisfied.

I put on a green apron. A green bow tie.
At the Perkins across from the hospital
I serve omelets to the grieving.
Careful with decafs and whole wheats.
Careful to be efficient and distant.
Hoping to feel irrelevant.

On the west side, I sell pool tables
and there I adore the green—
lain over slate under bright suspended lamps.
Two dozen emeralds in the dark warehouse.
Step out to smoke and the sunburned fringe
of foothills is blinding. Dying
to spark in the dry heat.
Inside, no customers, no calls.
I roll long, slow bank shots on the fastest carpets.

My world sort of bumps and flirts and buzzes up
to the fall of oh one.
At his nightclub my friend Ali

installs three eight-footers
on the balcony over the dance floor. Black
chrome, upgrade fabric, upgrade cushions.

We play hundreds of games.
All the pretty shapes we make
to dispatch a black solid.
Most I love the clear field:
green object of the game.

Noticing how much coffee people drink.
How many poured black circles hover.
Plus coffee at the hospital. Coffee at the funeral.
In the middle of dinner rush, busser slips
carrying two full cup racks—each six by six—
held solid by three-pound frames of company green plastic.

Some things unfold in smaller time.
Yes, there's that same yard always
and drizzling birch finally
pisses over the garage. The space
we made for a kennel
planted and replanted after the dog went down
ultimately houses an engine—
ceded to the reedy margin
around that decayed setting.

Then there's slip, fling, hair lift time.
Eyes open wide, splayed-out time
in which the tiniest bright interval
offers this thought: it's a cartoon:
cups suspended above his sudden

flailing horizontal. But that
moment has a conclusion in which cups smash
on busser's face as the back of his head meets linoleum.
Then, I don't actually hear birds chirping
or see stars spinning over his damaged head.

Above the ice bin, next to the shelf of colorful tea boxes,
we hang a nice picture (from his high school yearbook?).
His face glares white in the flash.
He seems more surprised than usual.
A couple weeks later he's back on the floor, lightly
bandaged. Heading for the cooler to restock
the salad bar, I see him sitting in the break room.
He's taken down the photo
covered his face with a dollar.
He's holding a lit match.

Any place will burn.
Drive around the West any September
about a million acres are burning.
That September, on TV
the sky burned over and over.

On the phone dad's worried
the yard's in bad shape.

And I'm drawing again and again disastrous cups
suspended over the horizontal busboy.

And everyone thinks everything that stands
stands for something.

The too many broken   the not being
there that didn't just   fall.

Ali moved to Canada after deluded patriots
saw a Syrian and just started swinging. No one
came to his club anymore except federal agents.
One last night we played eight ball on the balcony.
He told me about the place on Vancouver Island.
The feeling he could already feel
of breathing there, like a cool steam.
Later that week I went back
to the closed-down club and repo'd the tables
instead of dousing and sparking them
which I seriously considered.

FUGUE SYSTEM

I had the idea that the world's so full of pain

it must sometimes make a kind of singing

Robert Hass

FUGUE

Hospital copter skates south above the river:
urgency and ease in its glide and rotor hum.
Out of town, a girl has given her arms
to a thresher, or a passenger
rests half through a windshield.

Once, a truckful of police with clear
plastic shields sped away from city center
past a row of shops over basement apartments
where tenants ring chimes and light
candles in shrines every day.

Once, this place was on fire.
Once, under water. Once, this place
hurtled through a sudden dream
of light and heat—in form, unprecedented
in matter, all becoming of song.

Tower chimes and no one fails
to adore its orchestration. Songs pass in light
traffic. Arrangements slide toward jaywalkers,
café loiterers. All surfaces tend
to beautiful noise.

When lovers set the glass pipe down
on the bed stand of the rented room
a shaft of streetlight plays smoke and skin.
They exhale and descend into body.
Pace and pitch evolve.

A pattern of days drawn like a bow
over strings. Round wind in the throat of an oboe.
In the street, a wash of sound.
The cathedral rings the hour.
I take steady breath. I come to posture.

RHENISH

for Jay Meek

Our seventh year of marriage, we bought a house
we couldn't afford, inherited a dying golden retriever.
We grew sunflowers whose cheerful faces

might bear our civic responsibilities.
Often, we lingered in the cool interior
teaching our daughter to fit shapes in puzzles

while we committed ourselves to learning the old masters.
To us, that summer, Schumann represented lost time—
an age effaced by generations, the sublime dust

of high cultural inheritance. We checked out records
and a book, hoping our nostalgia and middle-aged foreboding
would give way to an elegance that had always been east of us.

Obviously, we knew nothing—syphilis, pseudonyms.
Fear and blank-mindedness fueled his prayers for song.
Our predetermined sense of the classical

would never have allowed for Eusebius and Florestan,
his contemplative and impetuous alter egos.
We would not have guessed his manic depression,

longing for death, excluded from joy but for glimpses.
For me, to imagine his forbidden love, Clara,
the frustration of it, along with everything—

I couldn't say what I felt about our easy passages.
The life of Schumann had challenged me to sing
down hallways much longer and darker than my own.

When we finally read of his incarceration and ultimate
death in an institution, we engineered a gesture vastly unequal
to the life and work that inspired it: we ran

speaker wire to the patio and played the *Rhenish*
into a humid, stifling dusk. The music settled
in the overgrown yard, crept among our chrysanthemums,

hung in the lamp-lit alley where no one passed.
At the final crescendo, our daughter raised her arms
in our ragged garden patch. We joked that she understood—

Schumann's conducting had been described as ineffectual.
We didn't try to fathom innocence or the heartrending onset
of knowledge. What could we have said?

Heat lingered long past dark—distant lights,
sounds of the city, arc of sky, the turning planet.
The next day we would start Debussy.

Restless, I sat up wondering what
beautiful strains might be designed by one growing
without so much rapture and affliction.

I PUT UP A TRELLIS

over a crescent sidewalk. A previous
owner poured it around a pool
then removed the pool
so I have this crescent
in ample green and latent
imaginings about a teenage girl
who lived here. Also a boy
who was always over and only
her second cousin. Crescent and young

silver maple   half barrel
of geraniums and some   debris: a child's
pink pool   a watering can and turned-over
sprinkler. This is now   framed by a fence
and beyond   a pine then
far off   a bluff
in front of blue.

I just thought what's more beautiful than beautiful
second cousins—polarized by shared animation.
Summer in the bright heat and shimmer
then back together into dim rooms.
Everything direct between them: shape
and temper and texture of everything

to come.   A grid
of previous diving   now supports this
cap of gangly blood   -red leaves.
It's a plunge past   a tree to be
found. Waking   dreaming bare

feet on concrete then   immersion: some
coursing-through to this   arousal.

Look.   In the shade over the crescent path.
The little boy   shakes the new
      white trellis.

IN A CORNER

So all that time
I never pulled a chair over
to the fenced corner
where the cracking garage
abuts the alleyway garden
        The dead
bleeding heart flower—yellow
tangled with crisp
gray still
enough moisture to stay
upright but clearly
reeling—it's the first
to go every fall
            I saw / was nearly
unconscious at bar time
last night: Oktoberfest   all that remained
for the passing season
a reel of pleasure
into nausea   for the dying
bleeding heart
the clematis peeking
from the sunny side
of the fence sings sweetly
            Another blue
flower look at it
scale damp siding to
reach its dying sister
and crawl up her
last translucent leg:
are we are we are we
            we are
meant to go soon too

FOR HEARING AND NOT HEARING

This voice an irrelevant chime, wanting to
shine in the air around this daughter, but
her infected ears won't transmit.
There's light on her page. She's coloring flowers.

No doubt words can be tedious.
At last week's graduation a Catholic cardinal
ignored a sex scandal while
reminding the newly certified of their debts.

I learned one in every million spoken words
has twelve letters like recalcitrant or narcissistic and
that after hearing Debussy's *Voiles*
one critic called a vast array what another

called dog sperm. If she were old enough
for irony I'd tell our little girl to feel lucky
about her temporary "losses." But that's not right.
Last night she woke up crying in a panic:

I called down the hall to calm her as if
she could hear. I heard her vomit
then her crying rose up. I found her pale at the bed edge.
Lips too red: fevered. She worried she'd made a mess.

I held her, said then sang *this is nothing*, which is
roughly what registers. This morning her flowers
are always for someone: this for Erin, Nick, Mama.
She says their names clearly and extra loud.

A HISTORY OF INTERRUPTION

11/13/04—after Walter Benjamin,
Dmitry Shostakovich, and David Byrne

1.

After the election
my friend touched my black shirt
mustered the thinnest smile ever recorded.
Now my Claire coughs
in the next room otherwise so
quiet I can hear the adagio in pianissimo
on the kitchen radio tuned to classical.

Claire would've lost the election too.
At five, incumbency seemed a violation.
"It's not fair," she said, "and anyway
I don't like him voting for war."
She asked how he won and I told her
people saw differently. An hour later
it was entirely gone from her mind.

2.

Back to this page now after
warming apple juice in a sippy.
Tired and feverish
she's home from kindergarten playing
pattern games on the PC.
Her cough is high and croupy
a little bark but not a whoop.
At night if she can't stop
we're to take her in the car

with the windows down.
The blast of November air tightens the lungs
and stops the spasm.
When she finishes a pattern
enchanted melodies ring through the house.

Outside all the signs still on the lawns like history
could carry the world by little tabs.
That you can lose something important
on a Tuesday seems unfair.

3.

Back to this page now after
she asked for something sweet and greeted
my pear with disdain
and the refrain "you need
your healthy choices" drifts like sweet bells
on massive weather patterns
charted in millennial cycles.

A thousand years—a thousand thousand thousand:
Even dear Walter Benjamin's only so helpful.
Can a moment matter? Can a cough
sputter beyond the atmosphere
like broadcast news in deep space?
Can a family in its generations
apprehend matters of importance?
Why lie and rush ruin?
Is Shostakovich somewhere still translating

occupation to anxiety in the strings?
In today's newspaper
a writer loved his friend's war cartoons
so much he thanked the commander in chief.

What can a family apprehend?
It's lovely, Claire, being here with you
even today, even a room away.

A family has its brains and given
span—can pass questions along
and imagine history answering.

And now I've honestly remembered
that yesterday was my sister's birthday
and I didn't call. And Claire
really can't stop coughing
and asking anyway for candy
and anyway I think of Talking Heads
"what good are notebooks?" in
"Life during Wartime."

A history of interruption might end this way:
In electronic music. In a man saying
"be grateful" to a child
while the nations burst forth.

At the house party, the cellist was an arranged
distraction, an elegant bridge
between distant guests whose propositions, hesitant
and restrained, were like a gentle spice in the air.
Expressionless, efficient,
he seemed to save energy for a later task
that might demand real feeling.

Late, when he laid his instrument on its side
and prepared to leave, the fresh absence of music
like an answer on the tip of a tongue, I took more wine
and approached his wooden stand. Somehow the long
sloping belly of the cello had become the woman
I'd been impossibly wanting, her back arched as I'd imagined it,
one arm stretched over a resonance at her center.
I stared and swallowed and, after a moment,

retreated upstairs to a private room
where a stack of coats smothered a brass bed.
From there, looking out on the constellations of city night,
I turned my thoughts to the man I once lived with
who came from his room each morning with wide eyes, shivering,
almost shocked. Then he cleaned for hours.
I knew he wanted something, not from me.
Scientists postulate a minute place at the center

of black holes, a place of massive condensation
a place of conversion. Looking out, feeling far removed
from the other proceedings, the other energies

under the sky, I felt I could not hurry
back downstairs to run my finger along the cello's wooden skin
and say to the indifferent musician, "this is so
beautiful, what you do," for fear
of lifting into the sky without burden.

BLANK SYSTEM

Nothing that's quite your own

Yet this is you

Ezra Pound

FAILED MOVIE

After late driving
beam riddled in my mind and through my chest.
The way headlights adrift
from the freeway swept the pasture plain
I had this feeling
a recently harvested steaming field
glimpsed through light stray from travel.
I stopped and tried
to capture on digital
what rapid candles of industry were making me.
Parked at the end
of a ramp past Fargo
I walked to the center of the overpass.
Wait. Air. Stars
visible through gaps in silver clouds.
After a while, a van and motorcycle
approached from two miles out.
I shot a full minute
but it doesn't show, really.
You hear the wind rush and the trim engines pass.
You see for a moment
light trails
too pixelated
and green glare off the sign that says one
hundred to the border.
I felt perforated—honeycombed and waning.
I shot my face for five counts.
My eye made one white circle.

NERVOUS SYSTEMS

Theory has dark matter
dense as a sky full of dusty textbooks
sweeping after brilliant spheres.
Tonight I see sparks showering
down an industrial chimney.
Imagine love.

The welder perched   handled
fire for hours then imagine coming up
the drive. Invisible
to what he sees in the kitchen light
—appliances and children
like advertisements taped to a mirror—
he thinks he might
disappear. He touches the door
imagines love
and steps inside.

Thinking black, I walk at night:
there's a sweet lemon coating
on every city block. Objects
look weird in sulfuric light
and they are weird. Once
the only time in my life
I sensed my own size
in a deep way: standing
next to an enormous pile of bananas
in a brightly lit convenience store
in the murky window
behind the register I appear
                              muddled distorted
kind of man escorting the sun.

Damned are those so it goes
choosing out   it must be
not so much for disdain
as survivor fear   if the spirit returns
pale and luminous   dark
lines drawn into its former skin
trembling will assume.
From the reels of our lives
nothing counters
that black version's blanking.

Tonight there's a new design
on the door of my favorite café:
preppy girl's coffee swirls—
gazing across a table at a swirly-eyed boy.
They conduct a flow   some sweet idea
worlds launch in perhaps slightly over
-caffeinated swoons   the door
swings open   snow spirals in
and dust.

FAILED SURVEY

—Four p.m.: scramble up cement spillway
eye level with late geese

They flex and launch low
over open water before rising—

Birds I should've counted passed beyond hills.
Snow began its numerous flurrying.

Many things surprised me: blood, tracks, signs
of digging. Gunshots near the property.

Two women walked a trail, holding hands.
I startled them. Apologized.

Landing leaping strides
I measured the limestone creek bottom.

I tested a tangle of ivy and wild rose
until my forearms stung.

My toe struck the chimney of a buried building.
I tumbled to my knees, scraped

dirty ice from mortared brick and found
the structure sound enough to brace push-ups.

—gather breath   evening in full
I clear this property—

THE NEW DEVELOPMENT

"All the Upanishads are the cows."

Srimad Bhagavad Gita

It's been pastureland for a century
but these thirty foundations, these thirty bony frames
will be called River Hills.

The houses must be valuable—out of town a ways.
But the lots are small so it's easy to imagine
the tangled network

of neighborhood secrets.
Today, I saw an owner
move a red-flagged stick six inches toward the adjacent parcel.

Last Friday I saw two boys kissing in the shell
of what might become a den, the end
of that day's sun on the hand pushing the shoulder down.

I turned back, sat on a front loader
and waited while the sun sank.
After a while an engine turned

headlights made a maze of the framed-out dusk
and dust in the taillights
intensified the sky's last deep shade of orange.

I decided then: my two-bedroom River Hills estate would be
in the south circle, concrete patio facing the adjacent pasture.
Every cow name I've forgotten

—names for the white, the brown-red,
the black and white—I will learn those again in order to call
upon their nonchalance.

Even with cement mixers, power saws, kids slinging rocks
and firing BBs into the herd—
even at night when the highway lights

streak the pasture like sideways lightning
they keep their cool. They're simply cows, even when it seems
they should be edgy cows. Maybe they find it funny

like a carnival in town with tents and hoopla
or a toy of simple progression—
mechanical figures crossing and dumping and hollering,

structures rising. At night the fast movers
stop and go away. This one guy
comes and shuffles around.

POEM FOR MY PUNCH

Tonight it's a so-sad instance
of something-I-see-makes-me-feel
-okay: nearly
                whole   that white
reflection of our hot remnant
lays cotton shimmer on
chairs in wet grass   man
                 in the moon
that's hilarious

I've got children
dreaming misty forests
on second floor
                a woman says
she'll never stop
loving me
        my brother
          some boy
held me down 'til I swung
           man I could
not sleep after I can't sleep now I
feel real real I
feel one hot circle this
heat is some sun   inside

SIN TEN MILLION

Grant and Lyon are talking
in Grant's office
I think. I'm gonna get a
drink from the cooler in a cup
I borrowed from Grant
three weeks ago.

He said this morning he wanted the cup back.
Fuck it, I'm thinking
I'll just hurry
down to the cooler
with his cup. I'm shaky
in the morning. Thirsty.
I'm thinking
he'll never see me.

Cool hallway
in the gray light from the window
the gray light through the Catholic school
window at the end
of the cool hallway.

The cup is full when I realize.
I'm clearly standing there and the fountain
pouring up from the cooler
has just drizzled down
when I realize

that Grant and Lyon are talking
about how the framers
would've this and would've that
in Lyon's office not Grant's

and I'm standing in the frame
of Lyon's doorway
at the cooler. The cup
clearly full and
in my hands I turn
in the frame
in the cool gray
in the gaze.

THE OWNER'S GARAGE

for Jerry Keir

It's disconcerting
how he's hung a flyer
for *Universo*
over the tool bench.

The face of Dugès, half shadow
with that gaze that drops me in my grave.

And he saves blurred photos—
that dark shade
is a mother cradling her sleeping child.
It seems a mistake, a bad

setting of the lens, but something
about it complements

this grim workplace:
knotted beams and shredded insulation.
And what is he making
all night under the bulb?

His bench is stained.
His rags are soaking.

FOR REAL JUNE

> "It is the absence of God that then speaks."
>
> MAURICE BLANCHOT

> "The back, the yoke, the yardage."
>
> ROBERT PINSKY

Folding shirts I am Pinsky
arguing with Blanchot. Here I am, Blanchot
folding real undershirts—look, no

tags now just a printed decal inside the collar.
All the more shirt, Blanchot.
I don't know my mangles

from my obtuse angles. Here's a
shirt—shape smell texture.
And the summer light greened

even through two windows
on the old orange recliner.
That takes a while to write down

and I know: what's left?
Tip of the tongue feeling. I think I see
is more thinking seeing.

My new neighbor—just divorced
slumming and struggling in a rental
with bad siding and bats.

She walks to her maroon compact car
parked next to my gray compact car.
A sudden convulsion

in the four-block radius of dogs.
Endangered songbirds in the lilac appeal.
Eight shirts stacked on an orange recliner.

Yes it doesn't
stop. Yes elsewhere presses
threaten small fingers—elsewhere forces

restrain bodies small, medium. White
squares repose in a living
room. These are words for things.

The leaves would be prosaic
but for their sheer number. Cold wind swirls; raking crews
work constantly to clear outbuildings, rosebushes,
and dry fountain pools.

Those entering the grounds for the first time,
admiring the gates and turrets,
cover their mouths and shield their eyes from the dust.
Inside, lodgers stand at windows,

away from card games.
They run their fingers along the dusty sills and examine
the fractured air, edged and veined by fragile skins.
Some believe the images the leaves call into their minds.

They see another window,
the reflection of a dinner table set for celebration.
They see snow falling, dark falling, and believe
they've revisited a final moment.

They turn to the card table and say,
"I must have died at dinner, in a northern climate."
The players might nod behind their concealed hands, or might
not respond at all, having spent their own time

at the window tracing spinning arcs backward.
They concentrate toward all they nearly recall—
flavor of roasted meat, concern in the eyes of those hovering,
mouths moving as words fade into light.

Wind rattles the screens.
Leaves kiss the glass. Lodgers listen for any echo of a name.

Beginning sorry in the mundane watching my cat
with its claws spring a stuck closet door—I guess it knows
which latches don't hold but what can latch mean to a cat
or door mean? Beginning sorry in lack I know
time is going down in me: I feel it more
and more out of sight. Without leverage or purchase
I can't gain it.
I found a triangle of prairie along the tall walls
of a city aqueduct. A tangle of trees bound the street side
and a switching station closed off the end. No one
went there for days. The moon streaked over.
The sun streaked over. No one person crossed.
Time is going there in me—its own parcel.
The cat is in the closet. Only he goes there.
It seems useless to guess why he wants the smell of boxes
so I don't. The mold and spiders. His own hair. So I don't.
It seems useless sorry to try gaining this sense of presence.
Moments catch me but mostly they don't.
They bury themselves having sorry never been present.
There weren't parties while I was growing up
where adults laughed and shared each other's warmth
so I don't remember those and yet they have time. They
go. I did go with my friends onto a desert playa.
At night it was a bowl of mountain shadow heaped with stars.
I went with my friends there. We stayed up by a fire.
We each walked far into the darkness and turned back to see the fire.
We called and hollered back and forth to each other.
I met a soldier who told me he'd been alone in the desert.
I knew a man who knew a man who was building
the empty shell of a city in the desert just to look at it.
Sensing proximity in a new way we were perhaps nervous there
sorry. Nervous to begin then from there. Sorry

to have to begin with so much having already gone.
Down in me the empty places. Down in me striations
like mineral levels of memory prepared for solution.
Well down. Well gone. The city prairie, the triangle:
sitting there I saw not one person in many days
so now I pretend that is heaven. I am sorry exhausting
my remaining beginning having made so little and thinking
like mundane nervous and lack. Down in the city prairie
I will carry my time. If you want me again
look for me under your boot-soles.

FIVE YEARS AFTER WATCHING THE PERSEIDS WITH A FRIEND
for Marc Lundeen

This August, streams run high and fast
down from Mount Evans, many days bringing bodies.
Death by water is everyday news here. We all imagine it—
a careless moment before a fast sweep and pull,
the cold and confusion and the coming up.

More than that summer week at your cabin, the seclusion,
our afternoon drinking vodka on the quiet beach, nights
floating on separate rafts watching meteors leap away
from Perseus into darkness, more than what we said
about love and death, looking into the water,

I remember you dropping me off at my parents' home.
The car door closed and I walked up the drive, alone.
Wind charged the pines. The grass needed water.
It's become a photo to me: my simple form, back turned
head down. What could I have been thinking?

It's no use trying, my familiarities are so changed.
The shapes and colors around me provide
not even the memory of a feeling. In Salinger, sometimes
I find a recollection of our impossible situation,
the usual wish for multiple resolutions. But, friend,

it's tiring, straining to recall. Here, my balcony
overlooks a basin longer than the rest of our days.
Last night, I watched a moth struggling on the curb;
the traffic whispered *yes*. Rain fell and the streams rose.
We all looked west at the shadow of a mountain.